The Little Boy Who Couldn't Stop Farting

By

Geryn Childress

The Little Boy Who Couldn't Stop Farting

He'd fart and fart... and fart and fart

He'd fart while in school... he'd fart at
Wal-mart

He'd fart in the morning... he'd fart in the day

But mostly he'd fart when he had
nothing to say.

He'd fart on his dog... -he'd fart on his cat.

Once he farted on a horse, while wearing his favorite cowboy hat.

He'd fart on little girls,

He'd fart on little boys.

He'd fart on all the children that
wouldn't share their toys.

He'd fart by the week, by the day, by the hour.

He'd fart eating breakfast,

he'd fart in the shower.

He'd fart on the young, he'd fart on the old.

He'd fart in the hot, he'd fart in the cold.

He'd fart on his family, his uncles and aunts,

Even his little brother at restaurants.

He'd fart in the car... he'd fart on the train,

BRREUMMUHH!!!On a boat... -or on an airplane.

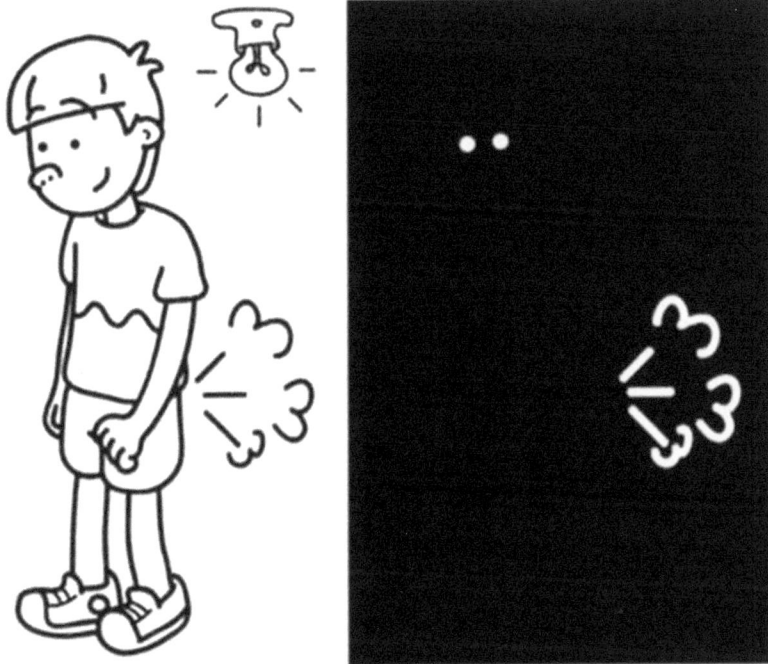

He'd fart and fart... and fart and fart.

He'd fart in the light, he'd fart in the dark.

He farted on all of the people he knew,

And one of these days he might fart on you.

Get The Whole Childress Children's Book Collection

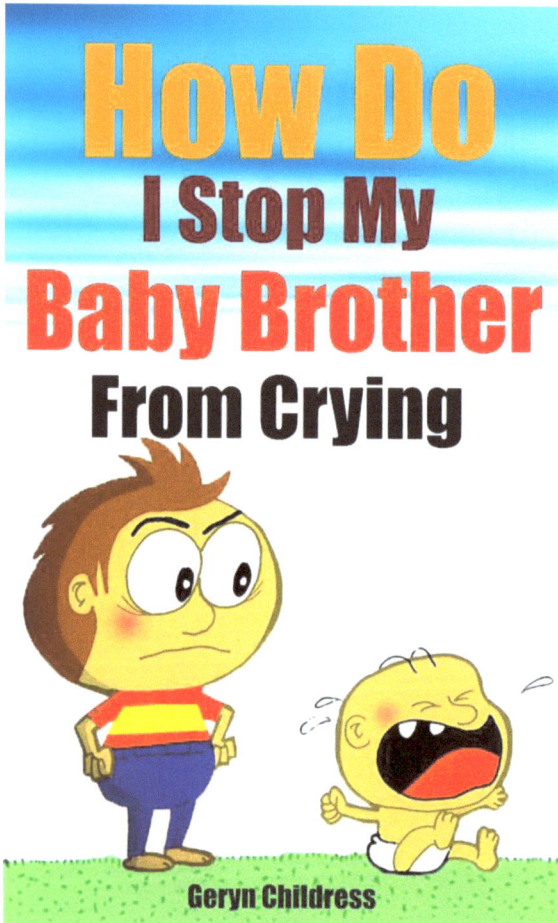

How Do I Stop My Baby Brother From Crying?

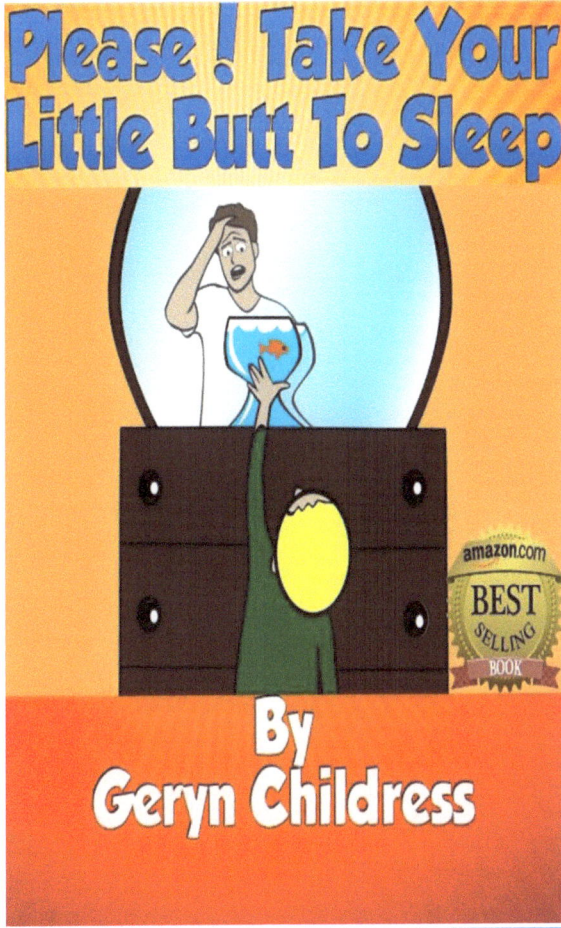

Please! Take Your Little Butt To Sleep

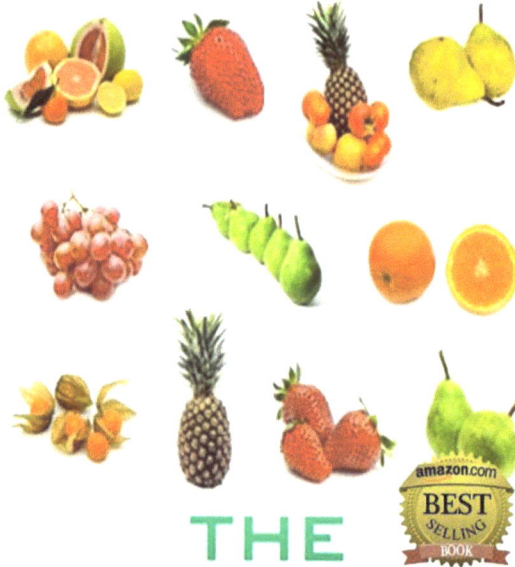

GERYN CHILDRESS

THE
What Am I?
BOOK

Collection of fun educational
riddles for kids and adults of all ages

Riddles:The What Am I? Book

Other Recommended Books

The Day the Crayons Quit

My Big Fat Zombie Goldfish

Dragons Love Tacos

Get All The Books In The Childress Children Book Series

http://www.childresschildrenbooks.com

www.ingramcontent.com/pod-product-compliance
Lightning Source LLC
LaVergne TN
LVHW010026070426
835509LV00001B/29